Pebble® Plus

Natural Wonders

Caves

by Kimberly M. Hutmacher

Consulting Editor: Gail Saunders-Smith, PhD

Consultant: Nikki Strong, PhD
St. Anthony Falls Laboratory
University of Minnesota

CAPSTONE PRESS
a capstone imprint

Pebble Plus is published by Capstone Press,
151 Good Counsel Drive, P.O. Box 669, Mankato, Minnesota 56002.
www.capstonepub.com

032010
005740CGF10

 Books published by Capstone Press are manufactured with paper
containing at least 10 percent post-consumer waste.

Library of Congress Cataloging-in-Publication Data
Hutmacher, Kimberly.
    Caves / by Kimberly M. Hutmacher.
    p. cm.—(Pebble plus. Natural wonders)
    Includes bibliographical references and index.
    Summary: "Simple text and full-color photos explain how caves form and why they are an important landform"—
Provided by publisher.
    ISBN 978-1-4296-5003-8 (library binding)
    ISBN 978-1-4296-5588-0 (paperback)
    1. Caves—Juvenile literature. I. Title. II. Series.
GB601.2.H88 2011
551.44'7—dc22   2010002790

Editorial Credits
Katy Kudela, editor; Heidi Thompson, designer; Kelly Garvin, media researcher; Eric Manske, production specialist

Photo Credits
Alamy/Clint Farlinger, 15
Dreamstime/Luis Estallo, 13; Mehmet Can, 11; Vinicius Tupinamba, 1
iStockphoto/Chris Pritchard, 7
Mary Evans Picture Library, 19
Shutterstock/Doug Lemke, cover; Nik Niklz, 9; PhotoSky 4t com, 21; Tatiana Popova, 5
Visuals Unlimited/Kjell Sandved, 17

Note to Parents and Teachers

The Natural Wonders series supports national geography standards related to the physical and
human characteristics of places. This book describes and illustrates caves. The images support
early readers in understanding the text. The repetition of words and phrases helps early readers
learn new words. This book also introduces early readers to subject-specific vocabulary words,
which are defined in the Glossary section. Early readers may need assistance to read some
words and to use the Table of Contents, Glossary, Read More, Internet Sites, and Index sections
of the book.

Table of Contents

How a Cave Forms 4

Inside Caves 10

Famous Caves 14

People and Caves 18

Glossary 22

Read More 23

Internet Sites 23

Index 24

How a Cave Forms

Water carves.

Earthquakes crack.

Over time, deep holes

form in rock.

These holes become caves.

Most caves form in
rock called limestone.
Water seeps into cracks
and dissolves the rock.
The cracks widen into holes.

Caves form in other ways.

Water running through ice

forms glacier caves.

Flowing lava can leave behind

caves called lava tubes.

Inside Caves

Inside caves, rocks

form works of art.

Water dissolves the rock floors

into shapes that look like

flowers and popcorn.

Icicles of rock fill caves too.

Stalactites hang down
from the ceilings.

Stalagmites stick up
from the floors.

13

Famous Caves

Kentucky's Mammoth Cave

is famous for its miles

and miles of passages.

It is the world's

longest known cave.

In New Zealand, glowworms

brighten Waitomo Caves.

Glowworms shine their bodies

in the dark to attract insects.

They catch and eat these insects.

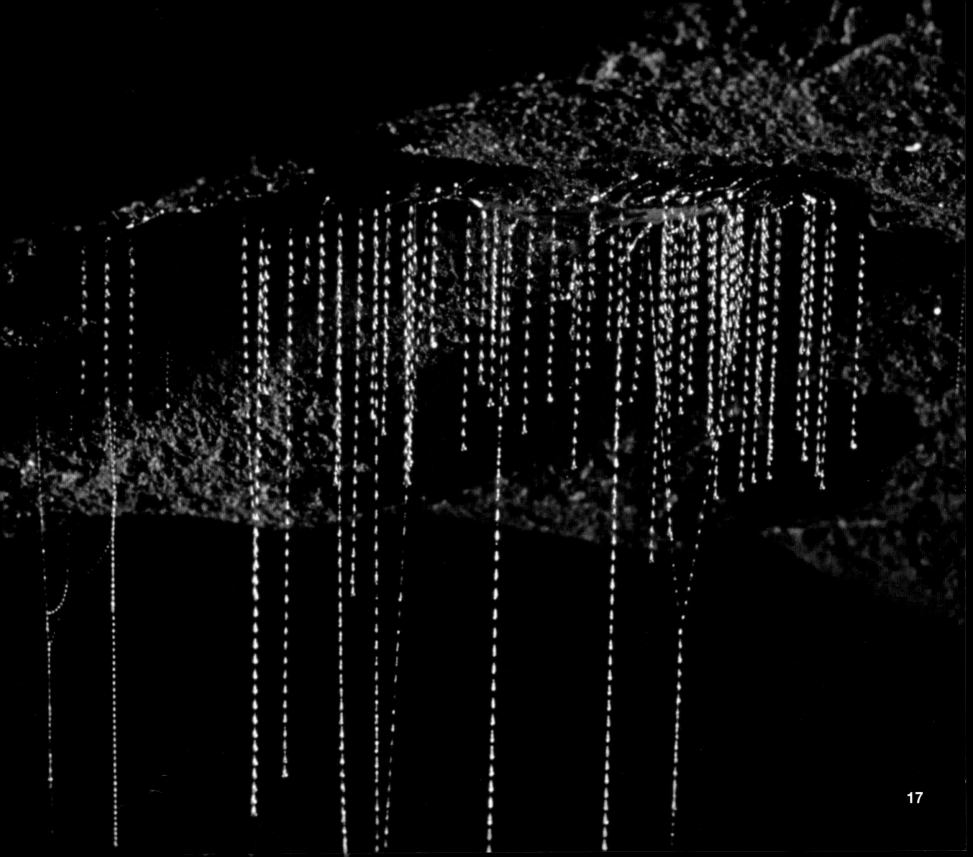

People and Caves

For thousands of years,

people have used caves.

Caves were hiding places.

People built homes

inside caves.

19

Today people study cave

paintings, such as those

in France's Lascaux Cave.

Caves help us learn about

life long ago.

Glossary

attract—to get the attention of someone
or something

dissolve—to break up when mixed with liquid

lava—the hot, liquid rock that pours out of a
volcano when it erupts

limestone—a type of rock that easily dissolves
in water that is a little acidic

passage—a hall or corridor

seep—to flow out slowly through small
openings or pores

stalactite—a long, narrow rock shaped like an
icicle that hangs from the roof of a cave; water
full of minerals drips and forms stalactites

stalagmite—a long, narrow rock shaped like an
icicle that sticks up from the floor of a cave

Read More

Dubowski, Mark. *Discovery in the Cave.* Step into Reading. New York: Random House, 2010.

Green, Emily K. *Caves.* Learning About the Earth. Minneapolis: Bellwether Media, 2007.

Internet Sites

FactHound offers a safe, fun way to find Internet sites related to this book. All of the sites on FactHound have been researched by our staff.

Here's all you do:

Visit www.facthound.com

FactHound will fetch the best sites for you!

Index

cave paintings, 20

earthquakes, 4

glaciers, 8

glowworms, 16

homes, 18

Lascaux Cave, 20

lava tubes, 8

limestone, 6

Mammoth Cave, 14

passages, 14

people, 18, 20

stalactites, 12

stalagmites, 12

Waitomo Caves, 16

water, 4, 6, 8, 10

Word Count: 173
Grade: 1
Early-Intervention Level: 20